Rank It!

MIXED MARTIAL ARTISTS

ELIZABETH NOLL

BLACK
RABBIT
BOOKS

Bolt is published by Black Rabbit Books
P.O. Box 3263, Mankato, Minnesota, 56002.
www.blackrabbitbooks.com
Copyright © 2017 Black Rabbit Books

Design and Production by Michael Sellner
Photo Research by Rhonda Milbrett

Library of Congress Control Number: 2015954677

HC ISBN: 978-1-68072-061-7   PB ISBN: 978-1-68072-267-3

Printed in the United States at CG Book Printers,
North Mankato, Minnesota, 56003. PO #1791 4/16

Web addresses included in this book were working and appropriate
at the time of publication. The publisher is not responsible for broken
or changed links.

Image Credits

AP: David Becker, 6 (Edgar), 12;
Corbis: Felipe Dana, 25 (Silva); Jeff
Haynes, 22; John Locher, 26; Flickr: Jeff Gor-
don, 6 (cage); Getty: Bob Riha Jr / Contributor, 8
(Gracie); J. Kopaloff / Contributor, 9; Josh Hedges/
Zuffa LLC / Contributor, Cover; Newscom: DC5 WENN
Photos/Newscom, 14 (Johnson); Jay Kopinski/Icon SMI
182, 15; Kevin Lock/ZUMA Press/Newscom, 19 (Miletich);
Rogan Thomson, 20–21; Rogan Thomson/Actionplus/
Newscom, 3; The San Diego Union–Tribune, 16 (Justino);
Shutterstock: A_Lesik, Back Cover, 1, 4–5; Andrey Yurlov,
32; dimair, 16–17, 24–25, 28 (banner); Martial Red, 6
(gloves); Natart076, 8, 13, 14, 23 (badge); nobeastsof-
ierce, 19 (cage); StepStock, 31; throwdown.com: 11
Every effort has been made to contact copyright
holders for material reproduced in this book.
Any omissions will be rectified in
subsequent printings if notice is
given to the publisher.

CONTENTS

CHAPTER 1

Into the CAGE

Two fighters step into the **cage**. They are ready for a fight. Mixed martial artists punch, kick, and wrestle. They give everything they have to win.

Mixed martial arts (MMA) fighters are tough. Turn the page to see how your favorites rank.

How to Win

1 submission—when a fighter has to quit

2 knockout (KO)

3 technical knock out (TKO)—when referee says it isn't safe for a fighter to continue

4 decision—when the referee decides who wins the match

CHAPTER 2

The

Frankie "The Answer" Edgar
fought from 2005–present

Frankie Edgar started as a wrestler. Today, he does a lot of **takedowns**. He's also good at boxing moves. Edgar won in April 2010 over B. J. Penn. That win is one of the most famous upsets in MMA history.

RANK IT!

6 WINS BY KO/TKO	**20-4-1** WIN-LOSS-DRAW RECORD
$2,798,000 ESTIMATED CAREER EARNINGS	**4** WINS BY SUBMISSION

(through 2015)

Royce Gracie
fought between 1993 and 2007

It was November 12, 1993. It was the first Ultimate Fighting Championship (UFC) tournament. A small fighter named Royce Gracie fought three times. He won all three fights. He used **jujitsu**. He beat men much bigger than he was. Because of Gracie, many MMA fighters use jujitsu.

RANK IT!

2 WINS BY KO/TKO

$400,000 ESTIMATED CAREER EARNINGS

14-2-3 WIN-LOSS-DRAW RECORD

12 WINS BY SUBMISSION

Randy "The Natural" Couture fought from 1997–2011

Randy Couture had a "ground and pound" style. He would punch an **opponent** who was on the floor. He won a UFC title five times.

RANK IT!

7 WINS BY KO/TKO	**19-11-0** WIN-LOSS-DRAW RECORD
$3,045,000 ESTIMATED CAREER EARNINGS	**4** WINS BY SUBMISSION

THE UFC CAGE

The UFC is one organization that holds MMA fights. People fight in cages against others of similar sizes.

UFC WEIGHT CLASSES

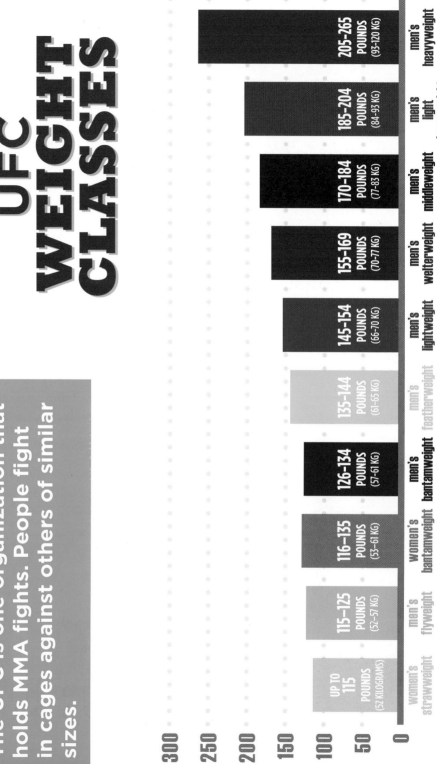

300	
250	
200	
150	
100	
50	
0	

UP TO 115 POUNDS (52 KILOGRAMS) — women's strawweight

115-125 POUNDS (52-57 KG) — men's flyweight

116-135 POUNDS (53-61 KG) — women's bantamweight

126-134 POUNDS (57-61 KG) — men's bantamweight

135-144 POUNDS (61-65 KG) — men's featherweight

145-154 POUNDS (66-70 KG) — men's lightweight

155-169 POUNDS (70-77 KG) — men's welterweight

170-184 POUNDS (77-83 KG) — men's middleweight

185-204 POUNDS (84-93 KG) — men's light heavyweight

205-265 POUNDS (93-120 KG) — men's heavyweight

30 FEET **WIDE**
(9 METERS)

6 FEET **HIGH**
(2 METERS)

750 SQUARE FEET
(70 SQUARE METERS)

Rousey is the first woman to win an Olympic medal in judo.

"Rowdy" Ronda Rousey
fought from 2011–present

Rousey's famous move is an armbar. She throws her opponent to the ground. She pulls the woman's arm back until the woman gives up. This move works. Rousey has won nine fights in under a minute.

RANK IT!

3 WINS BY KO/TKO

$1,300,000 ESTIMATED CAREER EARNINGS

12-1-0 WIN-LOSS-DRAW RECORD

9 WINS BY SUBMISSION

(through 2015)

Demetrious "Mighty Mouse" Johnson
fought from 2007–present

Demetrious Johnson's punches come fast. He's quick on his feet. And he has been called the best flyweight in the world. In his first pro fight, he knocked out the other guy in one minute!

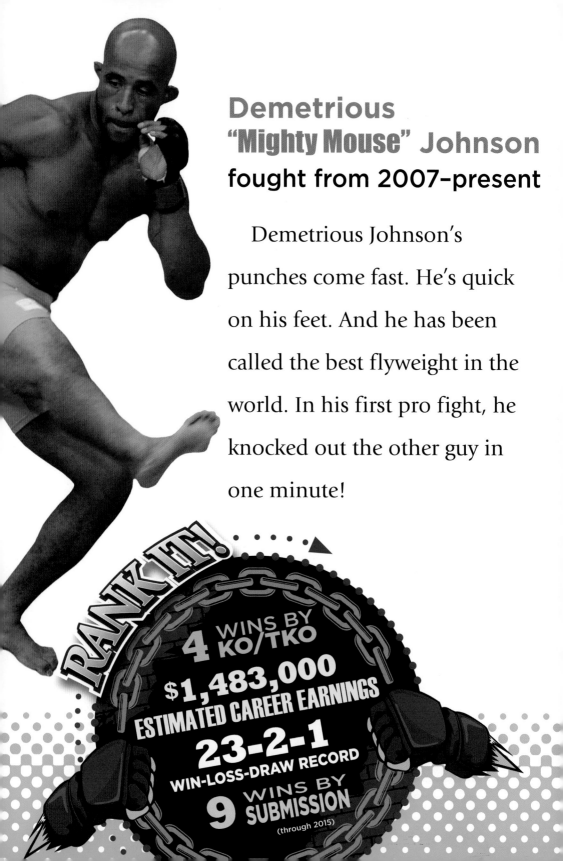

RANK IT!

4 WINS BY KO/TKO

$1,483,000 ESTIMATED CAREER EARNINGS

23-2-1 WIN-LOSS-DRAW RECORD

9 WINS BY SUBMISSION

(through 2015)

Tito "The People's Champ" Ortiz
fought between 1997 and today

Tito Ortiz started out wrestling. His wrestling moves help on the ground. He isn't afraid to go for a KO, though! He has the power to do it. He was UFC light heavyweight champion for more than three years.

RANK IT!

8 WINS BY KO/TKO

18-12-1 WIN-LOSS-DRAW RECORD

$4,135,000 ESTIMATED CAREER EARNINGS

4 WINS BY SUBMISSION

(through 2015)

RANK IT!

12 WINS BY KO/TKO

$388,000
ESTIMATED CAREER EARNINGS

Cris "Cyborg" Justino
fought between 2005 and today

Cris Justino won her first U.S. fight in 2008. She knocked out Shayna Baszler in the second round. But in 2011, tests showed Justino was taking drugs. She wasn't allowed to fight for a year. She bounced back, though. In 2015, she was a featherweight champion.

14-1-0
WIN-LOSS-DRAW RECORD

0 WINS BY SUBMISSION

Some athletes take drugs to make their muscles bigger. These drugs are illegal and harmful.

Pat "The Croation Sensation" Miletich
fought from 1995–2008

Pat Miletich helped start MMA in the United States. He was a UFC champion. He used the best moves from many fighting sports. He used wrestling, karate, and jujitsu. Today, he coaches fighters.

RANK IT!

5 WINS BY KO/TKO

29-7-2 WIN-LOSS-DRAW RECORD

$288,000 ESTIMATED CAREER EARNINGS

18 WINS BY SUBMISSION

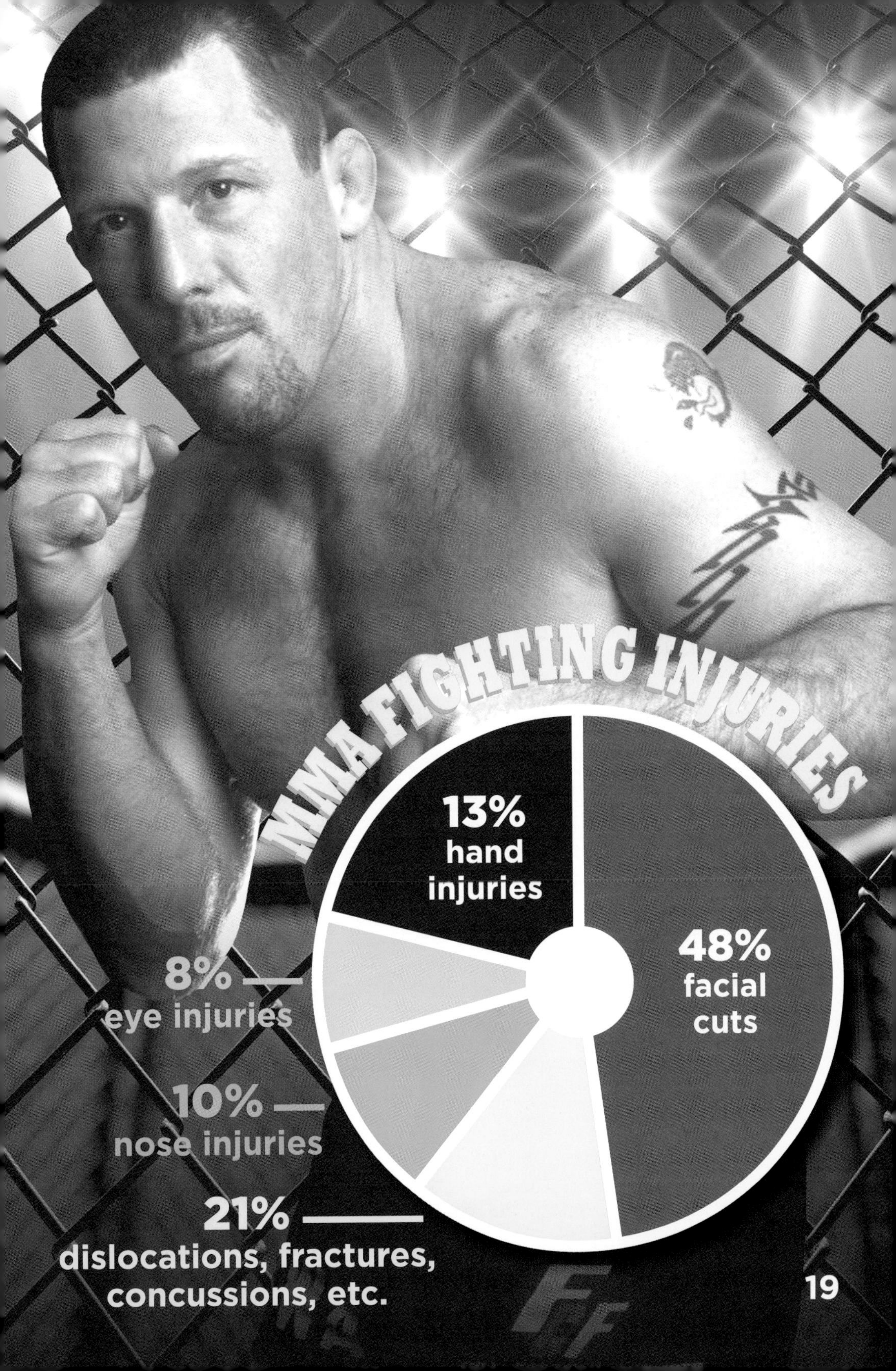

MMA FIGHTING INJURIES

13% hand injuries

48% facial cuts

8% — eye injuries

10% — nose injuries

21% — dislocations, fractures, concussions, etc.

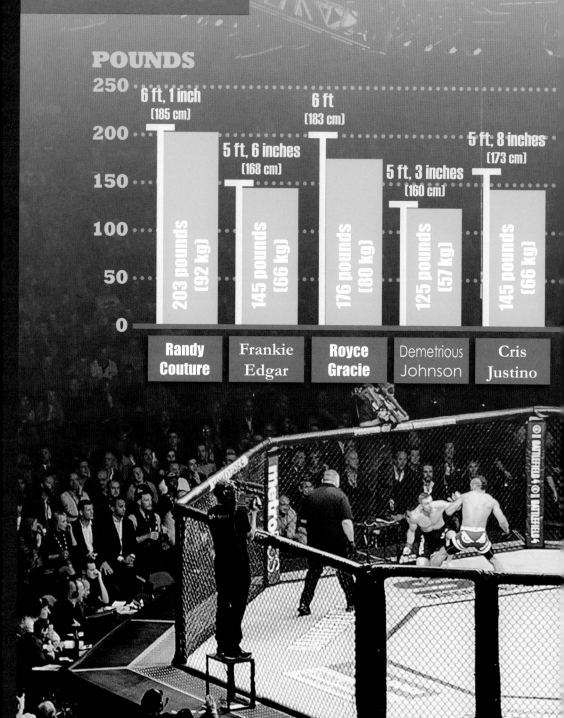

POUNDS

250

200

150

100

50

0

6 ft, 1 inch
(185 cm)

**203 pounds
(92 kg)**

5 ft, 6 inches
(168 cm)

**145 pounds
(66 kg)**

6 ft
(183 cm)

**176 pounds
(80 kg)**

5 ft, 3 inches
(160 cm)

**125 pounds
(57 kg)**

5 ft, 8 inches
(173 cm)

**145 pounds
(66 kg)**

| **Randy Couture** | Frankie Edgar | **Royce Gracie** | Demetrious Johnson | Cris Justino |

HEIGHT

6'6"

6 ft, 3 inches
(191 cm)

6 ft, 2 inches
(188 cm)

6'0"

ft, 10 inches
(178 cm)

5 ft, 7 inches
(170 cm)

5 ft, 6 inches
(168 cm)

5 ft, 6 inches
(168 cm)

5'6"

5'0"

183 pounds
(83 kg)

205 pounds
(93 kg)

135 pounds
(61 kg)

185 pounds
(84 kg)

135 pounds
(61 kg)

135 pounds
(61 kg)

4'6"

4'0"

| Pat Miletich | Tito Ortiz | Ronda Rousey | Anderson Silva | Miesha Tate | Cat Zingano |

Miesha "Cupcake" Tate
fought from 2007–present

Takedowns are key for Miesha Tate. She has power on the ground. Tate trained in wrestling and jujitsu. She was a women's bantamweight champion in 2011.

RANK IT!

3 WINS BY KO/TKO

$464,000 ESTIMATED CAREER EARNINGS

17-5-0 WIN-LOSS-DRAW RECORD

6 WINS BY SUBMISSION
(through 2015)

Anderson "The Spider" Silva
fought from 1997–present

Anderson Silva is known for his powerful hits. He won the UFC middleweight championship in 2006. He **defended** the title for a record seven years. Some say Silva is the best MMA fighter ever.

RANK IT!

20 WINS BY KO/TKO

$4,717,000 ESTIMATED CAREER EARNINGS

33-6-0
WIN-LOSS-DRAW RECORD

6 WINS BY SUBMISSION

25

Pay-Per-View Buys

Fans pay to watch UFC fights on TV.

86,000
pay-per-view buys in 1993

0
pay-per-view buys in 2000
(UFC wasn't allowed
on pay-per-view)

5,054,000
pay-per-view buys in 2007

3,205,000
pay-per-view buys in 2014

6,350,000
pay-per-view buys in 2015

"Alpha" Cat Zingano
fought from 2008–present

Cat Zingano is known for her punches. In 2013, she beat Miesha Tate by TKO. It was the first time a woman did that in the UFC. In February 2015, Zingano lost to Rousey. It was her first UFC loss.

5 **WINS BY KO/TKO**

9-1-0 WIN-LOSS-DRAW RECORD

$182,000 ESTIMATED CAREER EARNINGS

3 **WINS BY SUBMISSION**

(through 2015)

CHAPTER 3

Wins by KO/TKO

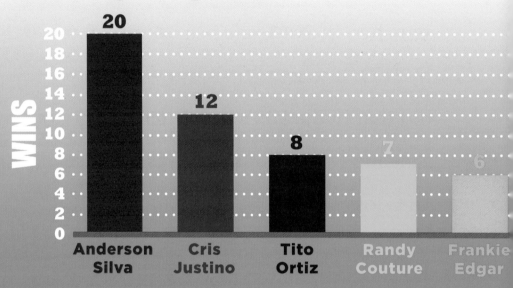

Wins by Submission

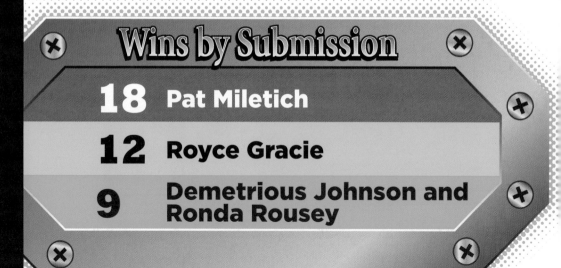

18	**Pat Miletich**
12	**Royce Gracie**
9	**Demetrious Johnson and Ronda Rousey**

RANK IT!

See how the greats stack up.

Pat Miletich	Cat Zingano	Demetrious Johnson	Miesha Tate	Ronda Rousey	Royce Gracie
5	5	4	3	3	2

ESTIMATED CAREER EARNINGS

$4,717,000 Anderson Silva

$4,135,000 Tito Ortiz

$3,045,000 Randy Couture

Win-Loss-Draw Record

ANDERSON SILVA
33–6–0

DEMETRIOUS JOHNSON
23–2–1

RONDA ROUSEY
12–1–0

29

GLOSSARY

cage (KAYJ)—a ring or fenced area where MMA fights are held

defend (de-FEND)—to fight in order to keep something

judo (JOO-doh)—a sport developed in Japan where players throw or wrestle each other to the ground

jujitsu (joo-JIT-soo)—a Japanese martial art

opponent (uh-POH-nunt)—a person, team, or group that is competing against another

takedown (TAYK-down)—a move that brings someone down to the ground

BOOKS

Castellano, Peter. *MMA*. Daredevil Sports. New York: Gareth Stevens, 2015.

Johnson, Nathan. *Kickboxing and MMA*. Mastering the Martial Arts. Broomall, PA: Mason Crest, 2015.

Jones, Patrick. *Ultimate Fighting: The Brains and Brawn of Mixed Martial Arts*. Spectacular Sports. Minneapolis: Millbrook Press, 2014.

WEBSITES

Discover UFC
www.ufc.com/discover

MMA Facts: The History
www.mmafacts.com/index.cfm?fa=main.history

INDEX